Risking It

Sylvia Byrne Pollack

ISBN 978-1-952204-09-8

Printed in the United States of America

RED MOUNTAIN PRESS
Seattle, Washington
www.redmountainpress.us

For Molly

Contents

Risking It

If it's confidently proclaimed,
a name for this large orange

mushroom glistening in rain
beside a Galiano Island trail,

does that make it safe to eat?
Is it better simply to admire

its vibrant copper flesh,
the way it binds raindrops,

stands alone in a patch
of small ferns and grasses?

Suppose a mycologist quotes
genus and species, shows

drawings in an atlas, will it be
tantalizing enough to take this lush

fungus into the kitchen, sauté it
with shallots, make a risotto?

These are the questions
faced every day: who to trust,

what to eat, how to prepare
for death.

How the Deaf Woman Hears

The deaf woman hears with heart   intuition   curiosity.

Conversation is improv.

She hears a word or two   thrown into the room by some
unidentifiable voice.

That becomes the nidus   focus   center
around which a sentence crystallizes in her mind.

This is called *fill in the blanks.*

This is called *hangman's noose.*

The rules are constructed of jello, overcooked spaghetti.

Flexible, open to interpretation and interruption.

The deaf woman invents continuity, acts as if she understands.

This is a ruse   sham   subterfuge   trick   wile   con.

It is exhausting.

The exhausted deaf woman tries to comprehend
grasp what is said   follow the thread of conversation.

She heard this can lead to depression.

DEAF-ISH

The deaf woman is not legally deaf.

According to the statutes she is hearing impaired.

Her pair of ears is imperfect.

For her there is no difference
roar of ocean   freeway
hiss of waterfall   escalator.

When she listens to music
she fills in missing notes from memory.

New songs have irreducible   gaps.

When the deaf woman reads about goats, she hears
Yudl ay EEE Ooooo

Rodgers and Hammerstein tune climbs Alps
pyramids   Himalayas   Seattle Space Needle
Cape Canaveral rocket gantries   Notre Dame spires
dangles from rock faces   gargoyles   flying buttresses.

It climbs up   over   down   into the sulci of her brain
echoing yodel-like   over and over   with no waning of sound
no fading away   just a merry-go-round
lonely goatherds and lovely Swiss misses.

WHAT THE DEAF WOMAN SEES

The deaf woman sees trouble wherever she looks
in front   behind   to the sides   up above   beneath.

She sees it in the future   the past   right this moment
sprawling and ugly.

It slobbers and snorts as it pries open her eyelids in the after-
midnight hours.

It rouses the deaf woman from sleep
dulls her senses.

She senses her dullness.

The deaf woman sees people selling their souls
their grandmothers   their firstborns   on the open market
on the world wide web   at community swap meets
in frenzies of "free trade."

They are busy buying   selling   texting   tweeting
don't notice their rights being amended   shortened
hemmed in   curtailed   trimmed   tazed.

The people are out-foxed but blithely insist
they still own the chicken coop
even while it and their national parks are given away.

The magnetic pull of the spectacle is too strong.

She can't look away.

FLAGRANCE

Our cherry tree was sick — girdled by
larking teenage boys, bark cut so deep

sap couldn't flow between roots and leaves.
Yet in its final year, before we had to cut it down,

that tree put out such an extravagance of blooms,
produced so many cherries, there were enough

for both the crows and us. Dying trees do this
an arborist explained — create as much fruit as they can

potential progeny to keep the lineage going.
Even cherries cultivated solely for their clouds

of pink and white spring flowers will shout
a last *banzai*. When the Tohoku tsunami roared

in on waves that topped a hundred feet, traveled
inland six miles in some places, it destroyed

people, houses, temples, highways, trees.
Brine shrimp and automobiles were flung

like offerings at the feet of Tohoku's cherry trees.
Those not ripped out on that March day

were soaked in brine, pickled like *umeboshi*.
Nothing could save them. And still,

they mustered what they could, commanded
hunkered buds to open in great billows

otherworldly in their ghostly beauty
to blot out desolation, decorate despair

a flagrant rapture of blossoms.

PRAYER FALLING ON DEAF EARS

Dear God
Please send a decoder, an angel
with mellifluous voice to perch
in the rim of my ear. Make her

multi-armed so she can catch,
parse and juggle the staccato bursts
of racket, soaring sibilants that pass
for human speech.

Let her have a device to analyze
the incoming cacophony, assemble
syllables. Give her an algorithm
to detect possible words (in English),

try them out for meaning in the context
of a rapid conversation.
What I'm saying, God, is that she
must be fast, perceptive, imaginative

and indefatigable. Try her out
on those words. If you can't
detail an angel to me, perhaps
you can put video displays

on the forehead of each person I meet.
Like supertitles at the opera, their words
will scroll gently across
riding the wrinkles.

If you'll do this, I promise
to stop nodding inanely, laughing
or looking serious at the wrong time.
I will be a credit to your handiwork.

if you decide to answer me, God,
please stand squarely in front of me.
Let me see your lips
when you speak.

Ever Hear Wolves ?

The *why-bother* bug is virulent this dark time of year.
It passes the blood-brain barrier, latches onto receptors

for dopamine and oxytocin, blocks feelings of reward,
of love. *Why-bother* is mediated by cytokines

and fun-house mirrors, distorting "what is." Goldilocks'
porridge is lumpy and cold. The wolf's teeth fall out.

Jack and Jill enlisted, went off to kill foreigners. Little
Bo Peep's flock was rendered redundant by tofu

and seitan. In Mexico, caravans of blind mice march
north toward the border, striking terror in elephants.

You're not asking for advice but I'd just like to point out
this will be your 80th February. It always gets better.

CLAMOR

Letitia sends her mind outside
to play quietly in the mud
hoping it finds buried treasures
pieces worth the wait.

Instead, it races frantically
a squirrel in the branches
of the walnut tree outside
the living room window.

Inside, projected on a blank wall
shadows cavort like Javanese puppets,
tell stories of kings and elephant armies,
cock fights, lovers, jesters.

She searches for the remote
to shut off the accompanying
surround-sound cacophony
mad blend of golden oldies radio
cell phone ringtones television
news shows podcasts symphony
excerpts movie soundtracks
conversations on and on
clamoring inside the husk of her head.

There is no remote.

CHASM

She gets through
another day, beyond
the desire to pound
her head against a wall,
to feel something.
To stop feeling.

Back from the brink
the chasm that suddenly opened
like a bad disaster film's
yawning faults, cows
and children flailing,
falling in.

Letitia wonders
what's so funny
about cows
somersaulting
mid-air?

LETITIA'S LOST BALLOON

She attempts to meditate,
        breathes in, breathes out,

watches her breath, feeling
        her abdomen rise and fall.

Then she remembers the shattered
        dining room light fixture.

Jagged edges of thought slice
        the narrow cord of her attention.

Her focus floats away, untethered
        balloon. She blows up another,

breathes in and out, two cycles
        this time. Then the car intrudes —

when can she get that hanging side mirror fixed?
        She recommits to the breath,

to the act of meditating but
        on the next exhale it's gone.

Come back, she calls
        to the minuscule balloon.

MEDITATION INSTRUCTIONS

※

Chant *home,* one hummable syllable.
Make chords with the relatives,

breathing in, breathing out. Everything
is here — anger, fear, love, ennui.

A cat prowls beneath the bedroom
window, crooning like a Tuvan,

under- and overtones bridging
the gap between species.

※

Concoct a soup from chicken bones,
parsnips, garlic, cayenne.

Pharmacopeia for the soul
om remedy for the deep ache

the loneliness of sentience
of being in a body and at sea.

※

Home is the sailor, humming
a shanty, the words risqué.

It's all a risk anyway.
Opening the lips to kiss

or sing lets microbes in.
Resistance is futile.

If the cat has your tongue,
let her keep it. Hum along.

The Hero's Journey

is now available as a package tour
    sponsored by AARP and your alumni association.

It begins with a wide circle out from home base
    through wild mountains and their dubious

inhabitants (Sasquatch, Yeti, Samovily, Shanhu)
    through desiccated deserts, random encounters

with camel-riding Bedouin, small oases, brilliant rocks.
    Then onward through snake-infested jungles

where scampering monkeys taunt bright-costumed
    tourists, snatching water bottles, biting them open.

Until at last, somewhere in the Southern Ocean,
    drifting dangerously close to Antarctica,

a hurricane carelessly tosses your cruise ship
    from crest to trough of 30-foot waves.

Over the PA system, the Russian captain intones
    Do not worry. She is strong ship.

Confined to your cabin, fed by a crew member
    tossing sandwiches from the doorway,

you ride the storm, take videos through a rollicking porthole.
    You will show those left at home the fury and sound.

You come safely to harbor at the tip of a continent
    that's drifting at the same rate your fingernails grow.

The lack of a manifest seems destined.
    You have only today, this shirt that's your favorite.

SPELUNKING

Grab a line —
    drop
        down

    into passages
    where images
    float, almost seen

        barely felt
        as they brush by,
        tinnitus of possible

            meanings singing in your ear.
            Explore the branching
            left   right

        until you squeeze at last
        into the curious chamber
        where ceilinged glowworms

    spell words
    bioluminescently

    and revelation

        cascades

            from

           ancient

            cliffs.

VAGRANT WALTZ

It's time in mid-summer
to think about nothing
turn from ideas

make ice cream instead
float on a raft of popsicle sticks.
You'll know when to get up

wield pencils like chopsticks
tease apart vagabond thoughts
meandering through your mind.

When bedraggled ideas knock
at your door, don't turn them
away. Like your mother before you

give handouts to hoboes
a sketch of a cat will be
etched on your gate.

Words will come tramping
into your dreams, vamp
your domesticated mind

with rumbles, a jungle
utterly outside your
safe picket fence.

ALONE, ALMOST

Is that *a lone wolf* or *signature loan* or simply
alone, except for the comedy duo Ms. Givings
and Ms. Apprehensions, splitting sides,

taking them? It's primary season, choices
must be made — to stick with the pack
or strike off on her own, ramble as far as

a gimpy hind leg will allow. Safer here
with those bound by genes or allegiance
to Mozart, Miro, and Szymborska.

Out there, where Buffalo and Rochester roam,
the music thumps. Lyrics of lost love and
loneliness stutter like stacked greeting cards,

dealt from the bottom of a barnacle-
encrusted deck. Abrasiveness of being
alone. And the solace. No one to disagree,

disappoint, disappear except on days
she is lost even to herself, drifting above
all she chooses to call real.

TAPAS

Not a real meal, no slabs of roast beef
slathered with gravy, no whole ears of corn
or canned green beans with almonds. Instead
we're surrounded by plated Picassos, strange
morsels, bold colors, odd angles, staring eyes.

The dishes keep coming. We point and say
that one and that one. Even the gristle
goes into our mouths, is chewed on. I take
a piece out, behind my cupped hand, hide it
under the rim of my plate.

Some things must be swallowed.

A neighbor dropped dead in his bathroom,
another just started chemo, all to the clucking
of the neighborhood chickens, loudly announcing
this Thursday, the only one we have. Their eggs
will transform into Spanish omelets, be boiled

or deviled, whipped into meringues, arranged
on the table in sundry small dishes beside
heirloom tomatoes and beans from our garden.
And onions that make us laugh at their exuberance —
how gracefully they shed their layers.

Kiss

Trellised tomatoes
        splay across the south
side of the house
        get drunk on their own sweet juices
stew in them
        grow so boisterously when it rains
after dry days
        skins split like opened zippers
and we in an act
        of compassion and forgiveness
pluck them off the vine
        offer them to each other's lips.

MOSSY LIMB

When passing by places where birds were sold,
[Leonardo DaVinci] would often take them out of their
cages with his own hands and set them free in the air.

—Giorgio Vasari (1568) *

I love how the words *mossy limb* feel in my mouth
dropped jaw of *moss*, then a slight smile as *limb*
lifts from my lips, mirroring Mona Lisa as she
recalled a Florentine woman, fair as she herself
was dark. Each came to sit in Leonardo's studio
for a husband-commissioned portrait, then stayed
to dally or slipped away, met in some nearby
bosky dell, made each other smile.

This spring, Bewick's wrens snatch moss from our
magnolia's trunk and branches, build their bower
on the back porch, match Leonardo in architectural
skills but reject his distaste for procreation.
They breed zealously, then, follow Leonardo's advice,
release fledglings to a world of dells and limbs and lust.

* *Lives of the Most Excellent Painters, Sculptors, and Architects (Le
Vite de' piu eccellenti pittori, scultori, ed architettori)*

Making the Bed

She makes it clear she doesn't need my help.
Or want it. Easier to do the job herself

tugging sheets onto this bed I bought
more than thirty years ago, good sturdy

Scandinavian design, a storage drawer
beneath the side that's mine. We've changed

the mattress from time to time, rigid
slabs of latex foam but now I need

something more forgiving, something to cradle
stiffened joints, sciatic pain. Perhaps it's time

for one of those adjustable memory beds
each side independently controlled, solo

choices in the night, moving silently
beside, not toward, each other.

ANNIVERSARY SONG

Listen, Love,
what I wanted to say
dissolved in this afternoon's
plummeting rain. Lord knows
we need rain but the timing
was off. No umbrella,
words written in chalk
on my hand.

Listen, Love,
what I meant to say
has already molded —
overripe cheese, fuzzy peach
in the back of the crisper drawer.

Listen, Love,
what I might have said
is in the pants press
I gave to Goodwill.
What I should have said
was festooned with blossoms
garlands of fuchsia crepe-
paper petals.

Listen, Love,
what I will say is
I'm heating the leftovers.
Supper will be
on the table at six.

APERTURE

That day I stumbled and fell, I wanted to know
    if I looked as disheveled as I felt.
My only mirror was a puddle, run-off

from a lawn sprinkler, trapped
    in a shallow depression in the macadam.
Clear water reflected my face

and peering over my shoulder
    was a white cloud, bandage on blue
covering a gap in the galaxy.

It was something like a hole in the air —
    not exactly but close enough that I decided
to put up curtains, give the air

something to push against, to frame
    the view — mountains, cows, interstate highway.
Hole as viewpoint, hole as devourer of hearts and lungs

(those great bellows that force air in and out,
    the mouth and nostrils holes in the air)
but this was not like lips or nares or curtained window.

This was the letter "O" singing arias
    in a medieval cathedral,
encompassing octaves.

This was the opening of a mind to the wonder
    of quadratic equations, of musical counterpoint,
of a well-wrought sestina.

This was a morning on Walden Pond
    carefully noting which plants had bloomed today
which seeds were released from the trees

floating or spiraling,
    carving serpentine holes
in the air.

GREGORY

I remember the day I picked up this rock
because he spoke to me (however he did that)
saying he was a particular piece of my past
I needed to take when I moved back to the city,
not pocket-size, like most of my beach finds
pebbles, glass shards and baby crab shells
but a substantial stone, liftable,
yet damn hard to carry all that way
from Possession Point to the cabin.

❀

He says he's named Gregory like the Great Pope,
kneels now on a small Persian carpet
on the floor of my study
not an ounce of anxiety in him.
He fills the room with presence,
chants in a humble monotone.
Is what I hear when I sit and am quiet
a congregation of molecules dancing,
tingling cymbals of silica?
Or is this plain chant, monophonic old song?

❀

His theology is so 7th century.
The desert monks taught him forbearance,
how to live with the 8 evil thoughts,
hold his own against lust and etc.
But Gregory has trouble with acedia
just can't bring himself
to get up and get going.
He sits there, distracted.
Beautiful mudflows slip through his thoughts.

It's time to recite matins, but he figures
there's always tomorrow.

⁂

Gregory regales me with tales of his relatives.
He gloats over the Pyramids,
exults in stone fences that mark out
sheep-dotted fields in Ireland.
He prefers stones like himself
with no artifice
though he greatly admires sculptors,
says Michelangelo is one of his heroes.

⁂

He grows wistful when he describes
tall stones standing upright in henges.
They've told him of magic,
adventures with little people,
celestial happenings.
And, of course, there's The Stone
that sealed up the grave for three days.
Gregory says that The Stone says
that he rolled away by himself.
It was hard.

⁂

When I ask how he learned
all these stories, he regards me oddly,
tells me we all might hear them
if we could be silent enough,
draw the slow twisting tales
out of the ether.
Jung knew about that.

Gregory's stoned, again,
shit-faced, groveling at my feet.
I forgive him.

It must be hard to be always so contained
the exchange of molecules with the air
so slow that it is possible
he has never taken a breath
in all the eons of his rocky existence
not once sighed.

FROM SILENCE

Before museums   before chisels
Before operating systems   computer code   semaphores
smoke signals
Before migration   before flight.
Before fear   anger   jealousy   disrespect

Before tearing legs off spiders
Before webs and a sense of hearth
Before land splintered into continents
Before the seas erupted   begetting land

Before star stuff coalesced into a blue-green planet
Before our solar system   before our galaxy
Before the universe noticed the music of the spheres
And began to riff on it

There was silence

And in the silence
An impulse to connect
A desire to create

From silence   everything

Not Vertigo

Flick your head sharply to the right.
That's not vertigo you feel

it's not your otoliths playing congas
in your semicircular canals.

It's your soul practicing escape
from the body, learning

to somersault into space.
What you see from the corner

of your eye as your head
whips around is the rest

of yourself, the part
you're too busy to play with

on August afternoons.
Glance left and right

and left again.
They are watching you

all the souls cut from
the same bolt of lightning

same stream of energy
arrays of electrons and protons

glissading your way, waiting
for you to rejoin them.

BLACKBERRIES

Great Scotch thistles, six to seven feet tall,
and rampant canes of Himalayan blackberries
guard our shore retreat, roofed by alders,

abutting beach, logs and drying kelp.
Each year the winter tides erase
another fraction of the woods

someday will take this entire leafy grotto.
But for now it stands,
a hideaway between beach and cliffs

where I discovered how contemporary
is that archaic word *swoon*.
Fainted with pleasure

the waves inside my head
utter liquid languidness
blue heron stretched against the wind.

That evening on my beach patrol
I plucked the first tart August berries
and brought them to you.

ISLAND TIME

Out on the island I know how things mesh,
how the tides wash and rinse kelp beds
every six hours, rising then falling, shifting
month by month so summer's extremes
become the gentle sloshing of equinox.

On the island I know where to pick blackberries,
how to find the Good Cheer Thrift Store or a farm
with fresh eggs. I know which beach yields sand dollars,
where to dig clams, pick mussels. I collect
drift wood, boil crabs, compose a chowder.

Out here I've learned the patience of herons
studying light and shadow. They wait for
ripples, glints of light, stand rooted to one spot
only as long as the fishing is good.
They keep their own schedules.

From my cabin I look east at the hulk
of the mainland, glad to be where time
is elastic, stretches and snaps back –
longline trolling me through seasons
of decision and desire.

Iron Springs Aubade

Beyond the surf, the water flattens.
    Poker-faced Pacific holds all the cards
        deals them when she chooses. In our cabin

perched on a high bluff, the alarm clock
    jangles at first light. Nobody set it.
        No one wants to be reminded of time

yet the tide insists. In and out, mood rises
    and falls, strews flotsam and jetsam
        such beautiful words for debris.

Long ago at Iron Springs, despair
    wrestled with hope in a rundown cabin.
        Everything's refurbished now.

This morning, twisted pines on the cliff
    welcome housekeeper winds, tidying
        these early hours into a new day.

LETITIA'S MIXED STATE

Frizzante bubbles of mania
work their indelicate way
through the grey sludge.

She is California and Maine,
Alabama and North Dakota.
Bilocated. Bipolar.

If she fights it,
the wrenching worsens,
disappointment deepens,

the desire to accomplish
something — anything — haunts.
She goes through the motions

of an actual person
laundry, groceries, scrubbing floors,
making dinner

shuffling along in her
concrete-booted mind
all systems out of whack

clumsy, fumbling,
dropping things,
frequent trips to the bathroom.

She climbs the stairs
on her hands and knees.

DID YOU FAIL LITHIUM OR DID IT FAIL YOU?

Tiny elemental socket wrenches,
do a turn, sometimes for the good,

sometimes not. Beleaguered synapses
borrow transmitters, send frantic SOS

signals. No one's receiving. Meanwhile,
there's the longing for some semblance

of sanity, all the marbles cinched safely
in a small handwoven bag, none rolled

under the sofa or used as ball bearings
in a Rube Goldberg contraption. Invention

is necessity's step-daughter, waiting for her
chance to step out, step up, into a waiting

pumpkin. When the wheels come off,
and they will, lithium works frantically

to right the carriage. The inevitable ditch
into which everything falls is filled

with dank water, toads, milfoil.
Word is sent for some desiccant.

Word is sent for a sump pump.
Word returns empty-handed.

WORDS MAKE SENSE — IT'S IN THEIR UNION CONTRACT

✵

While I massage your feet, we wait for anyone to notice
the irony of 600 count sheets when sleep is only
a metaphor, too poetic to be taken seriously. You say
Time to sleep. What do you mean by that?

✵

Night shades and day shades on a palette that is your palm,
lifeline highlighted in green, a road on a Google map.
Just don't trip on the yellow bricks on your way out the door,
smoke and mirrors packed in that sorry overnight bag
held together with a long strand of dental floss, its tensile
strength like a human life unwilling to depart, clinging
to what is known – the worn-out body, spaces between the
teeth, between the teeth and the tongue, the tongue and
the cheek. It goes on until it doesn't.

✵

Have you noticed how a room entertains itself, but the walls
feel lonely? The ceiling and floor have work to do. Helium-
filled balloons bounce forth & back, floor to ceiling, ceiling
to floor. Messages on the balloons are written in an unknown
tongue, one we killed but by neglect or design no one now
remembers. Study the words before the gas leaks out.

✵

There is nothing poetic in *that* or *this*. Quaker words, planed
smooth by repetition and the pressure of silence.
I've already said too much. Drink the amber words,
the tiny insect bodies still intact.

IT'S NOT ONLY DON JUANS

who collect skillful lines,
polish them, rehearse them,
calculate responses. Poets
do it, too, in their lust

for you readers who delight
in completing metaphors
revel in discerning frissons
believing a poem was written
solely for you.

Seduction and sentiment are twin horses.
Which one you ride makes the difference,
whether you gallop or canter,
which stable you have to muck out.
Be sure to bring carrots, sugar lumps
and, perhaps, a small
leather-bound dictionary.

Why am I telling you this?
If you've come this far, you already know.
You've been let down before. A poem
doesn't call back or halfway through
the third reading walks out.

But there are the "keepers" — the ones
Mother promised, the ones that still
warm you after all these years.
You've made peace with the fact
that though you are just one among lovers
no one else relishes the words
exactly like you.

What the Deaf Woman Doesn't Want to Hear

The screams of drilling   of trees falling   water diverting
fracking   in national forests. All make the tiny bones
in her ears vibrate in pain.

The deaf woman forces herself to listen.

She turns up the volume on the TV   hears wails
of people and sirens   sees carnage caused
by an unhinged man with an unlimited supply
of automatic weapons and ammunition shooting
into the fishbowl of 20,000 concert goers.

The deaf woman cannot distinguish the trill
of her tinnitus from the shrieking sirens.

It is all too much.

Just like it was the last time and the time before that
and soon the next time as we manage to average
one mass murder a day in these Disintegrating
States of America.

No one should have to hear this   hear of it   hear about it
hear how it went down.

The mood of the country is sinking   sucked down
by a fair-haired fat baby latched onto the nipple
of America   sucking her dry   spitting up all over her
pleased with himself.

The deaf woman hears her own revulsion.
It holds her head in its hands.

WHAT THE DEAF WOMAN CAN'T HEAR

The deaf woman doesn't hear the screams
from the gas chambers.

The gas chambers are silent as far
as she's concerned.

But the stench is remarkable.

Interestingly, no one talks about it, a form of politeness
like ignoring the hiccup   the belch   the fart.

The camps are wonders of efficiency   debasement   sadism
torture   murder   with their tawdry tattoos   blue numbers
on forearms   stacked bunks in the barracks   rotten rations.

What comes next in my country?
wonders the deaf woman
the disabled woman
the disposable woman.

Sometimes It's Better

Beneath the bedroom's dresser drawer
nestled in fluff that was my skin,
azalea pollen, cobweb shreds,
antennae of dead ants, an earring glints.

One of a pair, its mate consigned
last month to the Goodwill bin, all hope
of reunion given up. By rescuing this lone
survivor, do I set myself up to re-mourn a loss?

Sometimes it's better not to ask *what if*?

What if the car that hit my grandson
had been traveling faster down the alley?
Or if he hadn't flown off the bike before
the car ran over, flattened it?

Let some things lie, gather dust, disappear.

Ghazal for Birdseed and Poetry

The concatenation of atoms that formed her
scatters, each electron charges into the future.

In springtime, scanned irises, each one an original.
Behind veils, blank faces, a flicker darts into the future.

Delightful dispersal, ungluing of each sticky wicket —
whoever tries to squeeze through enlarges the future.

Brief verdant flames before a rumble of ashes mixes
with lies, makes soap, scrubs memory, purges the future.

A waxwing flies over the land, far from The Flood, seeking
birdseed and poetry. What else recharges the future?

No dashing Morse code, just a slow amble of words.
A halo remains, stuns our eyes as we regard the future.

Old growth forest — cut it down or let it rot slowly?
No matter. Sylvan nurse log lifts new trees, merges
into the future.

SOUL PHYSICS

What matters isn't static.
See how gracefully it transforms

into ardent energy, plunging
like a convoy of penguins

into an ice-filled sea
foraging for their young

wary of lurking leopard seals
and killer whales

but taking the plunge
regardless.

So little certainty
except death

whatever that
turns out to be.

You may suspect it is utter cessation
yet hold the tender possibility

that someday you will be less precisely
here, recycled, not recognizable

put to use energizing
something that matters.

On the Way to the Vancouver Art Museum

After stubbing the toe of my sensible shoe
on the edge of a recessed utility plate,
pitching forward with nothing or no one
to grab, to stop my momentum, I slid

away from my body, up, to the right, joined
a flock of crows watching a woman
resembling myself, wearing my clothes
as she crashed to the pavement.

Her carcass struggled to sitting but slumped there
waited for her hovering awareness to seep back,
to re-inhabit crannies and crevices, solidify into
her usual quasi-unitary being. Then, I got up.

Split apart so easily by a simple fall. Why should it
be any different at my final disintegration except flesh
will not welcome me back? And I may be able
to slip into exhibits of French modernists at my leisure.

THE WATER-MOON GUANYIN
At the Seattle Asian Art Museum

There's something about his insouciance
        how he sits, legs relaxed, right knee up,
                elbow propped, hand dangling

left foot floating above the floor.
        His eyes look closed but I know
            he sees all.

A slim smile on his pressed lips softens
        the square face, while long-lobed ears
            reach for chants I cannot hear.

Around his neck, a 13th-century sculptor carved
        a necklace of small rosettes, echoes of
            the full-blown rose pinning the sash

draped across flowing folds of wood.
        A sign commands "Do Not Touch"
            but *he* touched *me.*

The museum guard missed that
        walked over
            handed me a pencil, hissed

No pens in the gallery.
        Too late. My heart opened
           poem already written.

THICKET

Through the thicket of ribs, a needle
probes the left side of a chest, slips

into a chamber. Scarlet pulses
into the syringe. Slows. Stops.

Over and over, the same procedure
on each of the waiting sisters and brothers.

Pooled in a fat fifty milliliter tube,
their blood cross-connects in a clot

dense as a placenta, pulls away
from the straw-colored serum.

It looks like mead. Sometimes it's nearly
half a cup if the litter was large.

That's enough to do experiments for
months, to report in a cancer journal:

"Serum from day-old San Juan rabbits was used
as a source of cofactors for these assays"

not having to mention small gray pelts,
immobile noses, stacked on a laboratory bench.

Girls Gone Wild

When she saw the bright splotches
on the radiologist's ultrasound screen

she knew enough to know it wasn't good,
that somewhere along the line of cells

lining a milk duct, something had gone
haywire. Exuberant, giddy cells spilled out

reminisced about how they used to make
milk in their youth. It dribbled and spurted

but that was decades ago. Now
these girls-gone-wild want

to take a road trip, reach
the lymph highway ASAP,

spend spring break traveling or
beached somewhere warm like her liver.

That's not a viable option, she tells them
so cut out the craziness.

She took her own journey to a spot called
resection, imbibed poisons weekly,

got tattooed, let people
aim thunder bolts at her.

She came back with a scar her oncologist called
disfiguring but she figured

it was healthy scar tissue, more bonded
than the sorority sisters that hung out there before.

I'm Nearer the End of My Life than the Middle

Long ago I studied bright-winged Cecropia moths,
their wingspans as wide as my hand. Petite eggs

hatched into ravenous, hairy black larvae, growing
plump on the leaves of my professor's cherry trees.

The larvae molted four times, instar to instar, crawling
out of their old skin each time. And they ate it.

With each stage the larvae grew bigger, brighter,
morphing to yellow and orange, becoming at last

over-stuffed, blue-knobbed, emerald caterpillars.
Compelled by their hormones, they spun

brown silk sarcophagi. And waited for winter
to transform their russet husks into spring's

multi-hued wings. Without a hard freeze,
that last step isn't triggered.

I have known winter. It came undisguised.
I could show you scars but I won't.

What matters now is this question: Why
am I still afraid to dance all night with my soul

to be drunk with her, to rip open the cocoon
and emerge?

Ars Poetica

The poem that declines to be written
because it is self-conscious, shy, cryptic

or shallow is a poem that must nevertheless
be treated with respect — like a wild goshawk.

Don't try to take off its hood too soon.
Let it rest in the dark as the two of you get

to know each other. Your voice is important.
When the day comes, let it fly, watch where

it soars. If it disappears into the forest, you must
let it go. But if it flies back, feed it.

BACK

Letitia steps

in front of

an oncoming truck.

She is grabbed

by the collar

jerked back

onto the sidewalk.

She is glad.

No one is there.

Would a T. rex or a Kraken Be a Better Pet?

In the designated area, Black Dog lets me off leash
to run, sniff, explore, chase rabbits out of magician's hats.

We collect the rabbits' tails to give to our unlucky friends.
Deep into dark woods, we plunge through thickets.

I ride his back. I carry Black Dog under my pith helmet.
His doggy scent mixes with sweat running into my eyes.

We get lost but we have each other. And a leash that could
be used for a noose. Or, to pull ourselves back, up

over the edge of this cliff. When we play, he leaps on me,
knocks me off balance. This is not my favorite game.

I prefer when we play fetch and he races off
after some hare-brained scheme I've concocted.

He may be gone for weeks, occasionally months.
But I know he'll return no matter what I do.

When he decides to come back, he comes.
His entrance may be as subtle as a Gregorian chant or

as raucous as a Sousa march. He whimpers, barks, growls,
howls, according to his mood. I listen. I do not applaud

or encourage him yet he plops across my feet
leans his whole weight against me as I try to stand.

I ought to call him Millstone.
We are in a marriage but there is no divorce —

just reconciliation, understanding, acceptance.
Over and over again.

Ripening

I am ripening now in an autumn orchard,
still juicy enough to make cider
both tart and sweet. Not yet
ready to drop into the dry
wheat-colored grass to wither.

How can it be that October is almost here
yet my mind's full of March madness
April's indecisions still fluttering like
pollinating bees around the
Important Questions?

And wanting, some days,
to have been a tomato.

THE DEAF WOMAN AT THE TURN OF THE YEAR

The deaf woman stares into the navel of New Year's Eve
picks out lint   tosses it into a pile of confetti
ready for midnight.

From an upstairs window   she sees   purple peonies
blue and silver fish   orange horsetails   embroider the sky.

She recalls the Revolution's 200th anniversary in Paris
fireworks thundering   car alarms blaring   thousands of
citizens reveling in the streets   spilling into   out of
the Metro.

Enthusiasms   unleashed   ran in packs
sank fangs into tourists   frightened the natives
slobbered.

The deaf woman detects similar excesses
not effervescence of champagne   but erosion of civility
the caustic drip of lies.

The deaf woman wonders how long
until a guillotine
bursts forth on the National Mall.

THE DEAF WOMAN, TIME, AND DEATH

Whether the deaf woman is feeling renewal   mania   or just a
New Year's jolt only time will tell and time is a remarkably
open-ended   close-mouthed   artificial construct
the awareness of which makes humans twitchy.

Time goes fast   slow   creeps at a pretty or petty pace
is immemorial or a fresh new day   flies likes an arrow
a bullet   an aerialist   plods through mud   wounds and heals.

The deaf woman has already lived most of her allotted time
on this planet.

She is eager to plan her next adventure.

The deaf woman searches online for a travel agent   trip
adviser   cruise director   flight instructor   wilderness guide.

She finds ministers   rabbis   priests   imams   monks   nuns.
They offer glossy tracts   flight insurance   parables about lost
baggage   conflicting descriptions of what to expect when
arriving at the afterlife.

The deaf woman swallows the explanations
with a large grain of salt   chokes   spits them out.

She wonders whether death will be salty   sweet
bitter   savory   piquant   sour?

Or will death taste umami, fashioned
from soy sauce and maple syrup?

The deaf woman is upset by the lack of experimental data.

All the available facts are anecdotal
stories told by those who left the normal realm
of consciousness   traveled down corridors
attended reunions   saw sights and lights   smelled smells
came back empty handed.

Who doesn't bring back a souvenir   a memento
a tchotchke   from the trip of a lifetime?

ROAD TRIP

Our eyes are stuck on the scene
in the rearview mirror

saris and sake cups, petri
plates, music stands. Even

the side mirror, where things
are closer than they appear

seduces. Something creeps up,
with its massive engine, big enough

to boost this whole kit and caboodle
to the moon or some distant planet.

Stop checking the mirrors. We are
fine. Let's be visionaries, staring

through the windshield, looking for
natives to clothe: breasts to cover

souls to save. What we are leaving
will get along splendidly without us.

The promise of life everlasting
unfurls ahead like a highway

gold-paved, enticing. Yellow brick road
made of Velveeta cheese

but it turns out we all are
allergic to dairy. There was

no way of knowing until we were
already awash in a downpour

of milk and the windshield wipers
couldn't keep up.

TOURISTS

Those who come back talk about
           the tunnel and the light. Details
vary, who or what they saw.
           Some insist they traveled far
met family and God, while others,
           stayed put in the room, watched frantic
doctors thump tube-threaded flesh.

They never bring back catchy-sloganed
           T-shirts or shot glasses. Remarkably,
there's not a single photograph or
           video despite the near ubiquity
of smart phones, selfie sticks.
           If only they would show a carousel of images
with GPS coordinates embedded.

These travelers tell us they can offer
           only words and words, they say,
are so inadequate. Still, they try
           with glowing, rapturous adjectives.
But data-driven skeptics will avow
           these trips are just a dying brain's attempt
at making sense of the unthinkable.

That's possible and yet our minds persist
           in asking *but what if?* We and Horatio
know there are undreamed-of things.
           Why not believe the notion that a soul
goes on, its energy conserved
           that physics and theology might partner
in a cosmic travel agency?

INTERVENTION: WHAT'LL IT BE?
Like everyone else, I am waiting for death to intervene.—Eric Pankey

Should I choose the oft-invoked delivery truck
laden with prime merchandise, rushing
to make a delivery, smacking me sunny side up
blood smeared like hot sauce?

Or pick an airliner drifting slowly off course
disappearing from radar until months later
small chunks of wreckage wash up on atolls,
my flesh already fish food, my bones scattered?

Perhaps a more gradual exit is preferable
dwindling into incontinence, oblivion,
body and mind reduced…
paltry vestiges.

Would it be better to surrender
to a saber tooth tiger, busily shredding bodies,
culling the weak or be sold into slavery
to that cruel mistress, cancer?

I'm not brave enough to saunter
in front of tiger or truck.
When the slaver beckoned
I ran like the devil.

For twenty-odd years, I have looked
out the window to see what comes
down the road for me.

Circling over my house
are raptors and delivery drones.

One has a package for me.

Facing Sunset

is different, of course, from gazing
at brilliant tropical mornings
with colors of mangoes and berries
streaking the sky. Or tracking

the gradual roll back of fog, mist
burning off as the sun works its way
down to the Northwest coast.
No, this is more a relinquishing

letting go of the rheostat, no longer
trying to control the light. Or the dark.
Just letting it happen, slow degree
by degree, the shifting of colors

and focus. The lovely word *dusk*
painting the undersides of cumulus clouds.
The final flare of color and light
as the sun dips into the sea where

today is extinguished, memories
elide and night's mystery floats
like a hand carved bentwood box
waiting to be opened.

HONEYED DAYS

I used to believe old age was absurd
expected to live hard and die early.
How astounding I'm writing these words.

You know that proverb about early birds?
I guess worms are okay if you're hungry.
I used to believe old age was absurd

a sedate minuet on a harpsichord
but even minuets can swing jively.
How astounding I'm humming these words

not laid out in a box made of pine boards
or just fragments, the rest up the chimney.
I used to believe old age was absurd

now enjoy honeyed days unfettered.
To some I'm the object of envy!
How astounding I'm thinking these words.

It turns out that life is a smorgasbord —
mortality, frugality, chutney.
I used to believe old age was absurd.
How astounding I'm singing these words.

The Apricot Tree

The apricot's in bloom again,
old gangly tree that crafts

a single fruit or two each year
yet decks herself in copious flowers,

eager for pollen although there's not
another tree for miles

to partner her. Still, she keeps
blooming year after year.

It's her nature, not a conscious choice.
She never thought *I don't do blossoms anymore.*

Deciduous, driven, her moss-mottled
branches intertwined like nests

she lifts her thousand blossoms
to the sky, says *Use me.*

Acknowledgements

Many people and organizations have nurtured this work. My thanks to Cancer Lifeline, Hugo House, Jack Straw Cultural Center, and Poets on the Coast for writing workshops, classes, and inspiration. I have been buoyed by writing with and critiquing from Kelli Agodon, Dianne Aprile, Elizabeth Austen, Miriam Bassuk, Sharon Bryan, Laura Cooper, Kathleen Flenniken, Wendy Graf, Tim Kelly, Roselle Kovitz, Jared Leising, Joannie Mackowski, Anne McDuffie, Peter Pereira, Susan Rich, Kay Spikes, Peggy Sturdivant and Bette Weidman. Great gratitude to you all and to the many others who have enriched my poetry journey.

Particular thanks to Sharon Bryan, Kathleen Flenniken, Molly McGee, Peggy Sturdivant, and Bette Weidman for nudging me and then the manuscript in the right direction over many years, and to my wonderful editor at Red Mountain Press, Susan Gardner, for patiently bringing the book into focus.

My family is at the center of all I do. Thank you, dear ones.

My thanks to the editors and publishers of the journals where the following poems appeared, some in earlier forms:

Antiphon: "Alone Almost," "Anniversary Song"
Clover: A Literary Rag: "Prayer Falling on Deaf Ears," "From Silence"
Crab Creek Review: "Risking It," "Not Vertigo," "Flagrance"
Floating Bridge Review: "Thicket"
Hobble Creek Review: "Blackberries," "Island Time"
Jack Straw Writers Anthology: "Ever Hear Wolves?" "Ars Poetica"
Mason's Road Literary Journal: "Gregory," "The Apricot Tree"
Pontoon Poetry: "The Deaf Woman and Silence"
Shaken and Stirred by Cancer: "Girls Gone Wild"
SHARK REEF: "Vagrant Waltz"
Switched-on-Gutenberg: "Meditation Instructions"
What Rough Beast: "What the Deaf Woman Doesn't Want to Hear About," "The Deaf Woman at the Turn of the Year"
Wild Roof Journal: "Ghazal for Birdseed & Poetry"
WomenArts Quarterly Journal: "Aperture"

This book is set in Gill Sans, designed by Eric Gill and based on the earlier 1916 font by Edward Johnston, "Underground Alphabet", designed for the London Underground.